Kudos for *WETIQUETTE*

" *Wetiquette* serves as the official rule book we've never had, and in clear black and white passes judgement on everything from wave priority to proper conduct between sets."
Evan Slater, *Editor, Surfing Magazine 2002*

" Lots of knowledge, lots of laughs. *Wetiquette* is a small, perfect, little book."
Matt Warshaw, *The Encyclopedia of Surfing*

" *Wetiquette* will amuse experienced surfers, and more importantly, smooth the learning curve for beginners."
William Finnegan, *Author / Journalist / Hell Man*

" Vermouth-free. Tumbled. Drought-stricken. That's Peter Spacek's deft look at the foibles of modern surfing. Dry, is what I'm saying. In the best sort of way."
Scott Hulet, *The Surfer's Journal*

Wetiquette

How to Hang Ten without Stepping on Anyone's Toes

An
Illustrated
Pocket Guide
to
Surfing Etiquette

second edition

PETER SPACEK

Published by Ditch Ink
PO Box 1856, Montauk, NY 11954
www.ditchink.com

Edited by Arden Chapin Spacek

PRINTED IN THE UNITED STATES OF AMERICA BY JS MCCARTHY PRINTERS

For information about
wholesale purchases and other Ditch Ink products,
such as Surf & Mirth cards and apparel, call 619 997-9474
or email info@ditchink.com

wetiquette

(wet-i-ket) :

1. water sport etiquette
that enables
groups of wave riders
to share a surf spot
with minimal friction,
mishaps or injuries.
2. cordial, respectful
interaction in the ocean
that creates an atmosphere
of camaraderie and
positive vibrations.

*This guide uses genuine surf lingo.
Please see glossary for definitions of any words
or phrases that are foreign to you.*

Contents

Introduction

The ocean generates countless waves every day, yet sometimes it seems there still aren't enough to go around.

The public's embrace of surf culture, a growing coastal population, the explosion of user-friendly surf craft and the enormous popularity of SUP's have put many new people in the water. Add this group to the legion of core surfers and you've got a traffic problem.

All surfers, at least once, have been yelled at by another surfer. It usually happens early in your surfing career, around the time you're getting confident. You've mastered standing up and are starting to lean into your turns. You venture out into bigger waves, better spots, and among surfers whose abilities you admire. You're feeling like 'one of the gang' when suddenly you're being singled out by someone who is clearly offended by something you did. You are told to get out of the water, or go home. You may be called a kook, or worse.

Your brain is spinning as you try to figure out what you did to have enraged this surfing brother or sister. You're embarrassed and confused and think that you may not know what you are doing after all. So you try hard to remember what you did before the dude got got in your face.

If you're lucky, he or she noticed your confusion and took the time to explain, however briefly, and perhaps unpleasantly, the precise nature of your surfing faux pas. If not, you go home, try to sort it out and hope you don't do it again... whatever it was.

Then one day you'll be surfing, and someone will do to you, the same thing *you* did on that memorable day, and it will all become very clear.

That's learning the hard way.

This guide to surfing etiquette will explain the unwritten rules that define wave rider priority, help you avoid ride interference, encourage mutual respect, minimize the chance of injury (accidental or otherwise) and have more fun on the water. Read on, and learn the easier way.

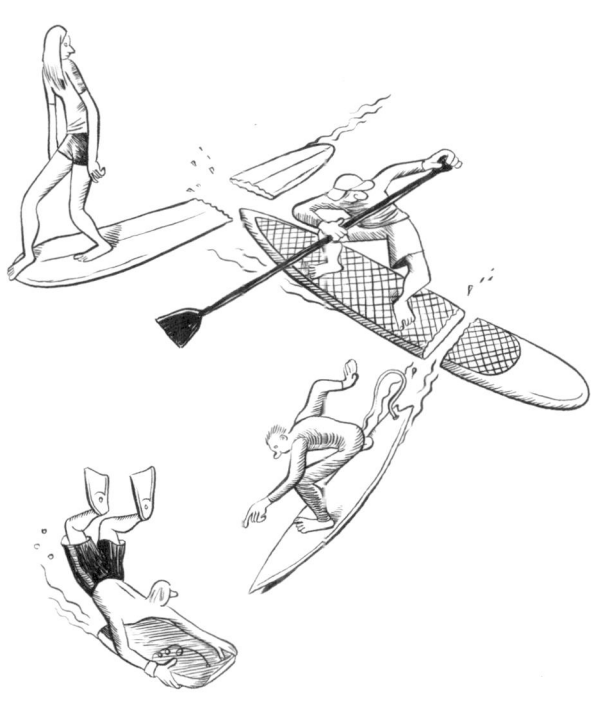

1. New to the sport

SURFING is an exhilarating and difficult sport. Learning the fundamentals is accomplished only through repetition – it takes hundreds of waves to turn a beginner into a skilled wave rider.

To speed up the process, avoid crowded 'name' spots. It's really hard to compete for waves with experienced wave-hungry regulars at the more famous breaks, and in addition to being discouraged, and possibly intimidated, you won't catch the waves you need to make much progress.

Practice among your peers at a known learning spot–it's more fun and you'll get better, faster. Seek out stretches of uncrowded beach break and get as many waves as possible under your belt, or... wetsuit.

When you are ready to tackle a popular break, go out for the first time when conditions aren't optimal (small, rainy, windy, etc.) Use the opportunity to determine the take-off spot and paddling channels. Then next time it fires, and the crowds are back, you'll be ready.

Most importantly, don't charge blindly into big surf, it takes time to develop the ability and fitness to confidently handle large waves. A familiar spot you think you know, can turn into an entirely different beast—big water moves faster and more powerfully, waves break farther out to sea in unpredictable ways, and rips and currents are stronger. Although rare, the possibility of drowning is real, and having to be rescued endangers others.

If you have any doubt about the conditions, ask a local. You'll get a straight answer.

2. Situations
You'll be surfing in these arenas:

REEF BREAKS,
and RIVER MOUTHS
Waves may break
to the left and to right,
allowing two surfers to ride
one wave at the same time
without conflict. The take-
off zone is usually constant
but can move with tide,
swell size and direction.

BEACH BREAKS
Sandbars and wind
swells create rideable waves
on a sandy bottom. Waves peak
and break in many places and take-off spots
move continuously. On a long stretch of beach,
it's entirely possible to find a peak to yourself.

POINT BREAKS, and JETTIES

This is where it's most difficult to secure rider priority. The wave breaks in one direction and the take-off spot is frequently congested. And competing for long, quality point break waves, tends to pump up aggressiveness.

3. Paddling Out

As you wax up, study the line-up. This is when you determine your paddling route. See where the sets are breaking and where the other surfers are sitting. The idea is to paddle out without getting caught by a wave and without getting in the way of a ride. Walk knee-deep into the water and stop. Wait for a lull and look around for other riders. If your paddling path is clear, go quickly. If you are caught by a breaking wave, try to punch through it. Do not let go of the board and roll off. An abandoned board, even when attached by a leash, is dangerous to you and anyone behind you– (*very* dangerous if that board is a heavier SUP) there are times in large and powerful surf when ditching your board is unavoidable, but in average conditions hold on tight.

COMFORT ZONE

4. Picking Your Spot

This can be tricky. You want to be in the best spot to catch a wave and so does everyone else. There's a loosely established order in place, which your arrival has disturbed. This is the time to be on your best behavior. Sit off to the side of the main pack and assess the situation. Do not sit too close—or in front of anyone. It's considered an affront, and can be hazardous because it doesn't give the necessary elbow room to sprint clear of an unexpected outside wave, or from hard-to-predict incoming surfers.

Use this time to study the waves. Are they peaking consistently in the same place? Or is there a secondary take-off spot? Determine where you want to sit—not too far inside, where you might have to dodge people, and not too far outside, where you won't be able to catch a wave.

Now wait for a set to scatter the crowd, and take advantage of the momentary disorder to move into a prime take-off position, all without encroaching on anyone's space or 'comfort zone'.

5. Wave Choice

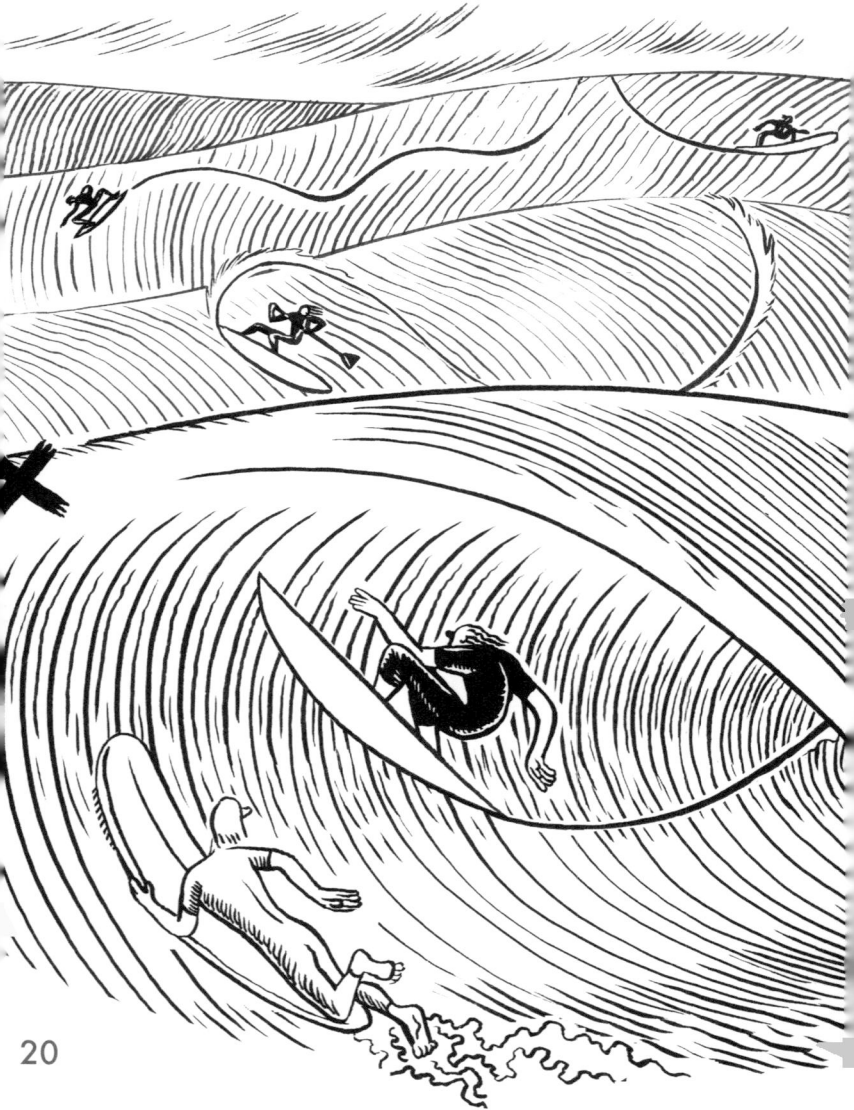

A set looms. Study the wave—is it feathering? Can you make it over? Paddle farther out if necessary. Avoid paddling across anyone's path, beware of others around you, and maintain the 'comfort zone'. Now decide if this wave is worth competing for. Determine how many others are going for it. Look for signs of a bigger wave behind it, there usually is one. If you choose to pass, get out of the way of others paddling for the wave.

If you're trying to get over a wave being surfed, make every effort not to interfere. Either hold back, and let the rider pass, or paddle quickly over the wave before he or she nears. You have to make that decision based on the surfer's speed, their direction, where you are, and what the wave is doing. And then, guess his or her next move.

Beginners commonly miscalculate, and paddle into the path of the rider. At best, it's a ruined ride. Obviously, it's better to hold back and take a hit from the breaking wave than risk a collision. In time, predicting, anticipating and avoiding will become second nature.

6. Basic Right of Way

Generally speaking, the person closest to the peak has priority. Since this is the steepest part of the wave, they will have been in position to catch it first, which confirms their priority with the 'First One Up' rule.

A peak that breaks right and left can accommodate two riders. To avoid possible conflict, ask which direction the other surfer is planning to go. If two of you are paddling for the same wave and you're not sure that he or she will catch it, ask them if they've got it. Conversely, if you don't think you're going to catch a wave you've been paddling for, encourage someone else to go for it.

Even though surfers can be tight-lipped, communication is appreciated, and creates feelings of good will.

7. Your Wave

You're stroking for a wave that you believe should be yours. You feel it picking you up and you're about to hop to your feet. Now, look over your shoulder, away from the direction you are about to go. Is there anyone already on the wave? If so, abort. Pull back sharply so you don't go 'over the falls' onto the rider. If you choose to drop in anyway, you will have committed surfing's worst crime. You've cut someone off. Before there were leashes, boards were routinely 'shot' at perpetrators.

8. Unexpected Company

So you've caught the wave and it appears to be all yours. You hop to your feet and drop down the face. Suddenly, there's a whistle or a shout, and you realize someone's already on it. You hadn't seen anyone, but now you're bumping boards.
Don't panic– exit the wave with a smooth kick-out.
Try not to fall off, if you do, it's highly probable that the other rider will also, either by collision or by sudden evasive action. Then the two of you will get your leashes tangled while floundering in the impact zone.

It can be a very awkward situation.
An apology would be appropriate and goes far.
Hopefully everything has gone as planned.
Other surfers have pulled back and given
you the wave, and no one has been
accidentally cut-off. You're free to enjoy
the ride. Have fun! But keep an eye open for
people paddling out, and be prepared to
change course to keep from

running over
someone.

9. More

You've enjoyed a clean ride. You're stoked and you'd like another.

Paddle back out while looking for incoming riders and try to stay out of their way, as others did for you. When you get back in the line-up, don't get greedy and stroke furiously for the next available wave. Surfers that hog waves will soon find themselves being dropped in on. If you're on a Long Board, or a Stand Up Paddle board, don't abuse your paddling advantage. Consider surfing in spots that are appropriate to your vehicle of choice—it's no fun getting the stink-eye if there are other options. When the waves come in consistently, and people are respectful and communicating and getting their fair share, the surf zone is a happy and relaxed place.

It *is* nice to find waves all to yourself, but it's also fun to surf in a group. Good-natured competition raises performance levels and there are others to learn from. And besides... if no one saw your four-second tube ride, who would believe it?

A final word.

The playing field isn't always level. Some people paddle faster. Some have uncanny wave knowledge that puts them in the right place every time. And some have the edge because they have the right craft for the conditions. And sometimes, you'll have a frustrating and unsatisfying session simply because there are too many people and only so many waves. It happens.

But a lot of the time, if you stick to the rules, you'll have days where everything comes together and magic happens—that exhilarating feeling of surfing a good wave, well. And that's just the beginning. So stay fit, respect Mother Ocean, ride her waves carefully and she will enrich your entire life. Now go get wet!

ewOooO

10. Random Info and Suggestions

(that may seem obvious to some.)

A SIMPLE **NOD**
and
👁 CONTACT
works wonders

If you're in a position to safely catch a loose board, do it.

Do not lay your board wax-side down onto the sand. Elevate one end. Do not lay your board wax-side up on warm days, ~ the wax will melt.

Learn to surf on a SURFBOARD before trying it on a S.U.P.

go green whenever possible

Do not walk trailing your leash, and do not walk with your leash attached to your ankle. Wrap it around the tail and secure.

Down-play wave height when describing conditions. The waves may be head-high, but eyebrows will be raised if you call it six foot.

5 ft.

While waiting for waves on a Stand Up Paddleboard refrain from positioning yourself directly in front of "conventional" surfers.

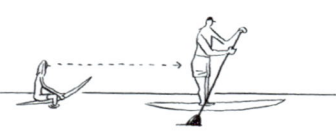

It's courteous to warn an unattentive person of a looming set of large waves.

RESPECT the LOCALS
they RIP

Out SIDE!

If you are cut-off, alert the 'perp' to your presence by whistling and/or shouting. Be careful doing this if the person appears large and/or dangerous.

Hey you! YO!

Good surf etiquette is understood world-wide, but there are still places defended by aggressive LOCALISM that are exceptions to the rule.
GO HOME

Good surfers get more waves. It's a law of surfing nature, and one of the reasons they got that way.

my wave.

Don't paddle out with dry hair

Unless you want to trumpet your arrival.

KOOK
is an ugly word

Give a wave to a surfing Senior whenever you can

IN A NUT SHELL
SHARE AND PLAY NICE

Glossary

barrel	the hollow inside of a breaking wave. *tube.*
barreled	to have ridden inside a wave, in the *barrel*.
board, shooting	to propel a surfboard, while riding, at another surfer.
caught inside	to be unable to paddle out to sea in time to avoid a wave before before it breaks.
cut off	to interfere with a surfer who has priority by riding in front of his or her direction of travel.
drop in	to start your ride down the face of the wave.
dropped in-on	to have unwanted company join you on a wave.
feathering	a wave starting to crest.
firing	a surf spot at its best, with numerous high quality waves.
going off	see firing. also used to describe hi-performance surfing.
hoot	an 'awoo' sound used to express approval.
impact zone	the area where most waves initially break
inside	the area in the surf between the beach and the impact zone
kick out	to end a ride by turning your board sharply seaward
kook	an unskilled wave rider, derogatory.
leash	a tether or cord connecting surfer to surfboard.
left	a wave peeling left from the surfer's point of view.
line-up	surfers holding position in the wave catching zone.
local	a regular at a surf spot, sometimes residing nearby.
localism	a ganging-up of locals (usually) who use intimidation to discourage others from surfing a particular spot.
long board	a rounded, stable surfboard around 9' long commonly used by beginners, but enjoyed at all levels.
lull	a pause in wave activity.
over-the-falls	to be one with the breaking lip of a wave, unintentionally.
peak	the highest point of a wave.
right	a wave peeling to the right from a surfer's point of view.
set	a group of several waves.

shortboard	a surfboard, 5' to 7' long, that turns easily, but requires a better wave and expertise to get up to speed.
shoulder hopper	a surfer without priority that *drops in* on others.
snake	to paddle around someone in priority position, just as a wave arrives, attempting to claim rights to it.
stink eye	a spiteful look meant to show dissaproval.
stoked	thrilled, happy, excited.
SUP	Stand Up Paddleboard. a large wide surfboard propelled-in a standing position, with a long single bladed paddle.
take-off spot	ideal wave catching zone.
tube	the hollow inside of a breaking wave. *barrel.*
tubed	to have ridden inside a wave. *barreled.*
wave hog	overly enthusiastic surfer that bogarts waves.

p s

About the Author/Artist

Peter Spacek grew up in Santa Barbara, California
surfing it's points and coves
(where he learned surf etiquette the hard way.)
And when he wasn't surfing, he was drawing pictures
about surfing it's points and coves.
He moved on to drawing for *Surfer, Surfing,* and
The Surfer's Journal, and more.
Spacek is now known for his humorous
beach culture cards, graphics and cartoons,
which are published by Ditch Ink
under the *Surf and Mirth* banner.
When Spacek isn't drawing, he's scratching.
In 2010 at OutEast Gallery, Montauk,
he unveiled his technique of scribing images
into old surfboard fiberglass and rubbing ink into
the scratches–a technique called *scrimshaw.*
For more about that, google him.
He has a wife,
(this modest book is devoted to her)
a daughter, two stepsons and a dog
who split their time between Eastern Long Island
and Leucadia, California
surfing and drawing
in both places (but not the dog).

PETER
SPACEK